OptimaLearning®

French For Kids

For ages 2¹/₂ to 15

Learn Along With Your Child

To all those who believed like the little blue engine:

*"I think I can, I think I can …
I thought I could, I thought I could."*

CONTENTS

Page

1	Introduction		
2	Before You Start		
3	Principles and Concepts of Optimalearning		
4	How to Use This Course		
4	Basic Lesson Sequence		
6	Pronunciation Guide		

8	Lesson 1	Bonjour	*Greetings, what's your name, my name…*
10	Lesson 2	Clown	*Face Parts*
12	Lesson 3	Le Chat	*Animal names, what is this?*
14	Lesson 4	Le Fête des Canards	*More animals, how do they sound?*
16	Lesson 5	Flic Floc	*Water, rain, frog*
18	Lesson 6	Polichinelle	*Body parts, directions*
20	Lesson 7	Papillon	*Where do you live, friends*
22	Lesson 8	Au Marché	*Counting, fruits, vegetables, shopping*
26	Lesson 9	Bon Appétit	*I'm hungry, meal time*
28	Lesson 10	Bonne Nuit	*Bedtime, good night greetings*

30	Activity Page for La Fête des Canards, Bonne Nuit
31	Supplementary Vocabulary

Cassettes

Instruction Cassette – Red Label

Tape 1 Side 1	Songs 1 – 6
Tape 1 Side 2	Songs 7 – 10
	Supplementary Vocabulary *(colors, polite forms)*

Reinforcement Cassette – Blue Label

Tape 2 Side 1	Songs only 1 – 8
Tape 2 Side 2	Songs 9 – 10
	Supplementary Vocabulary *(terms of endearment, washing up, praises, negative forms, commands, useful expressions)*

With special acknowledgement to Dr. Georgi Lozanov for his courageous and pioneering work in the field of accelerated learning, and to Dr. Ivan Barzakov for his vision and his special contributions in the field of mind development.

Special thanks to all those who helped to produce OptimaLearning FRENCH FOR KIDS :

Music and Lyrics, Guitar	Christiane Lelaure
Boy's Voice	Nicolas Malfroy-Camine
Flute	Ben Borson
Mandolin	Tom Sleckman
Sound Engineer	Lee Lusted
Dialogues	Christiane Lelaure, Pamela Rand
Phonetic Symbols System	Ivan Barzakov, Ph.D.
Artists	Cover Suzi Marquess (Whimsey Walls)
	Design Gwen Graham
	Drawings Lynn Miller Coleman
	Suzi Marquess
Methodology Consultant	Ivan Barzakov, Ph.D.
Consultant	Margaret Chambers
Marketing	Christopher Ireland
Photo	Katie Holt
Production Assistants	Helene King, Fran Rondeau
Editing, Typesetting	Margie Bajurin
Producer	Pamela Rand

INTRODUCTION

Congratulations on choosing this OptimaLearning® course for your child. This gift of early exposure to another language will build a wonderful foundation for language learning for both you and your child. Your child will have greater success in school and more opportunity at work in a global economy, if he or she can speak another language.

Why You Should Begin Exposing Your Young Child to Other Languages

Recent studies clearly show that the earlier you expose a child to several languages, the greater the child's mental development. Verbal skills, comprehension, and self-confidence are significantly enhanced. This special way of fostering both self-expression and the capabilities for language promotes future academic achievement.

Before your children can speak a language, they must be able to *hear* the particular sounds and auditory frequencies of that language, according to Dr. Alfred Tomatis (world-famous otolaryngologist and psychophysiologist). From the womb through early childhood, youngsters have a wide open sensitivity to a range of sounds. They quickly assimilate the accents, inflections and sound patterns of any language to which they are exposed. By the time children enter kindergarten, they know most of the grammar of their native tongue and its daily vocabulary. During this natural language development period, children quickly and joyfully pick up any language without conscious effort. Language permeates their activities.

During these early years, before the tongue and ear are conditioned completely to the sounds of English, a child can easily imitate the sounds of other languages, which many adults find difficult. Children's minds actually remember language in a different manner before the age of twelve, when biological changes in the brain make learning languages as difficult as it is for adults.

Neuron development in the brain is critical in a child's pre-school years. Stimulation develops neuron networks which in turn largely determine the child's ultimate physiological brain capacity. When children learn a second and third language, they are actually increasing their cognitive flexibility, a key to problem solving and creativity.

Dr. Tomatis demonstrated that *hearing* a language correctly is the most critical skill in language and learning development. Once children acquire this ability to hear the full range of another language, this capacity *remains* even if that language is unspoken for many years. When children begin formal study of that language in school, they retain the ability to speak with native intonation and accent, and are considered "gifted" in learning the language.

The Advantage of OptimaLearning's French For Kids

You do not have to speak French in order to share this special learning experience with your child or class. Incorporating the OptimaLearning method, this course is designed to allow even the non-French speaking parent or caregiver to teach the lessons correctly and confidently. The written text is presented in three forms: French, simple phonetics, and English. The recorded text and songs are all clearly delivered by fluent French speakers so that your child will hear the language spoken accurately. You can relax and learn together with your child in a fun and easy way.

Each lesson is carefully designed for the young child with an interesting conversation, a short rhythmical song, and vocabulary that the child will understand and enjoy. The songs and dialogues are recorded by Christiane Lelaure, and she is accompanied by Nicolas Malfroy-Camine. They are both native French speakers.

The following concise instructions introduce you to the OptimaLearning method and describe how to set up an ideal learning environment for your child. There are suggested activities for each lesson, along with extra vocabulary, and a suggested toy or other object that can enhance the learning process.

The **red-labeled cassette** delivers the individual lessons. The **blue-labeled cassette** presents the songs without dialogue, to provide a recreational reinforcement of the lessons. Both cassettes also contain supplementary vocabulary, introduced through a specialized accelerated learning technique of Reading with Music™.

Although designed for youngsters ages 2 1/2–8, this course can be enjoyed by children of all ages and adults too. If you have older children at home who want to learn French, you can enlist their help in teaching the younger ones. They can teach the new language while increasing self-confidence in their ability to learn the language at the same time.

Many mothers expose their newborns and, in some instances, their unborn infants, to the sounds and songs. Studies show that the fetus begins to "hear" sounds of the mother's voice at four months. This early exposure helps stimulate the brain and create optimal conditions for future mental development and ear training.

BEFORE YOU START

Before you begin, carefully review the following guiding principles and concepts of OptimaLearning. Become familiar with these principles. Think about how you can apply them in other ways in your parenting, caregiving, or teaching.

OptimaLearning® Environment and Ritual

Create a special OptimaLearning environment for these language sessions. This environment should be intimate, pleasant, and warm — a space where your child feels very comfortable. Select a place that has minimal distractions, such as a corner of a room or an area on the floor with the tape recorder nearby. If you choose the floor, you may want to use pillows for you and your child.

Another essential feature of the OptimaLearning environment is the *symbol*. This symbol could be a flag, a special doll, or some other item that symbolizes for you the culture of the new language (without being associated with any particular lesson). The symbol also serves as a signal that the session is about to begin, and helps the child and you to "shift" to another world. It should be put away at the end of each lesson.

Creating a special place and a ritual around the beginning of a learning activity helps the learner to mentally and physically make the transition to learning or working, and to retain the information longer and with easier recall. When you are away from home, be sure and take the symbol with you to maintain the link with the established ritual. As Dr. Ivan Barzakov, internationally recognized educational psychologist and expert in mind development says, "Encourage in your child ritualistic associations with the OptimaLearning environment which invoke the joy of learning."

Another aspect of the ritual is called the "alerting technique™," which aids the child in any transition. You "alert" your child whenever you give him/her a signal that you plan to change the activity. For instance, "When you finish eating, we're going for a walk." Or, "When you finish drawing that picture, we're going to listen to Christiane and Nicolas." By alerting your child, rather than interrupting his or her activity with an immediate command, you give the child a few brief moments to complete an activity and prepare for a new one. The ritual itself should help build anticipation and excitement about the upcoming language lesson.

OptimaLearning is fun. If you need to get materials or arrange something for the OptimaLearning environment, or for the suggested activities of a particular lesson, enthusiastically invite your child to help. "Let's get our pillows so we can listen to Christiane and Nicolas." "Come and help me draw butterfly wings for our French lesson." After a while you may want to begin speaking in French as you make the transition.

Remember to build anticipatory pleasure by reinforcing the child's competence and accomplishment. "You're learning so many new names for your face. Isn't it fun?" Or, "I love to hear you sing. Shall we learn a new song today in French?"

PRINCIPLES AND CONCEPTS OF OPTIMALEARNING®

Expectancy vs. expectation.

Expectations are your greatest enemies! Unconsciously, you will project them to your children, who will develop frustration and lose self-confidence when their learning occurs in a different pattern. As native speakers, we don't think about the word sequence of a sentence or the way we hold our tongue when pronouncing a word. These habits of thought and speech are assimilated over long exposure. When a child begins talking (between the ages of 1–3) he or she is bringing to the surface for the first time the result of hundreds of hours of listening, observing, and responding. When language activity begins, it accelerates at an amazing speed. But each child is individual in the pattern and sequence of his or her speech development.

Accept your child. Rather than forming expectations of a particular progress path, create for your child the sense of delight and expectancy to be found in talking in another language. Help your child get excited about learning.

Ritual.

As you recall, a ritual in this course is a specific action or object which always happens or appears at the same time (for example, at the beginning of a lesson, or at the very end). The significance of ritual and how to establish it is outlined under *OptimaLearning Environment and Ritual* on page 2. Another example of "alerting" is to take your child on your lap for a special hug and a quiet moment just before starting the lesson. Be creative and think of a ritual that fits your child. For an older child, you might both try closing your eyes as you narrate a brief magic carpet ride to France. Children love imaginative journeys.

Rhythm and Intonation.

Music has several special functions in OptimaLearning. The melody and rhythm provide an enriched framework for the memory. Children's songs are replete with repetition that aids learning as it provides a sense of the familiar. In this series, specially created songs will help your children learn and effortlessly practice new vocabulary. The clear teacher's voice with a simple guitar accompaniment is especially effective in its simplicity and intimacy.

Your own voice is also an instrument. Listen to its quality. Is it gentle and tender, inviting? Do you vary the pitch and timbre to create suspense and drama in conversation, as well as in story-telling? In creating an atmosphere of playful, happy learning, use your voice appropriately.

Educative Feedback™.

One of the keys to stress-free learning is Educative Feedback. The purpose of feedback in any system is to change future output. Feedback is neutral, non-judgmental and addresses performances, not the person. Thus, it is fundamentally different from criticism or correction in human relationships.

Educative Feedback differs from feedback in general through its special emphasis on building a sense of self-confidence. In language learning this can be achieved through the technique of "layering," along with ample support. "Layering" means that you will not directly interrupt or correct your child or children when they make mistakes. Instead you will encourage their responses in the new language and find an opportunity to substitute a better (more appropriate) model *without* labeling or calling attention to error. Remember to always encourage the child's expression and participation, no matter how unsatisfactory it appears according to your criteria. When supported and encouraged, your child will be very quick to adjust to the "correct" pronunciation.

Receptivity.

Learning is optimal when all levels of the mind are open and receptive to what is taught. This occurs when learners are **excited, encouraged,** and **accepted.** Several components of the Optimalearning method help create these conditions of receptivity. As we discussed, these are expectancy, ritual, rhythm, intonation, and especially Educative Feedback.

A few additional tips:

Relax and let the tapes provide the initial models in the OptimaLearning course. As you feel comfortable, engage in verbal exercises with your child. Don't be inhibited by your own lack of knowledge or fluency in the new language.

Avoid memorization. You did not learn your primary language through memorization. Exposure is the key. Your child is a natural language learner. Don't turn a lesson into a drill. Touch on the points and move on. There is always another opportunity. Meanwhile, don't underestimate the unseen learning that precedes spoken words.

Flow with your child's own pattern of learning. Use all the senses. Encourage your child to touch, move, look, sing, speak, even taste.

HOW TO USE THIS COURSE

- Familiarize yourself with our simple phonetic system to assist you with pronunciation. Take it easy. Don't be overly thorough – in time your mind will absorb everything. As Dr. Georgi Lozanov, psychiatrist, educator and father of modern accelerated learning says, "Allow a certain amount of the information to come through unconscious learning." Above all, be gentle with yourself, and playful – no one is going to test you.
- Create an OptimaLearning environment with all its components.
- Preview each new lesson before going over it with your child.
- Read over the Activities Box of each lesson and gather the necessary materials for the exercises you choose that day. Whenever appropriate, prepare the optional object as a prop for that lesson.

Your preparation is now complete.

BASIC LESSON SEQUENCE

(These cassettes are recorded in Dolby Stereo.)

ADVANCE the red-labeled cassette to the lesson you are studying.

INVITE your child to learn, and build expectancy (as previously described).

OPEN the book to the appropriate lesson to follow along while you play it on the tape recorder.

LISTEN to the short dialogue. Point to the picture to help your child make connections. For example, in the clown song, parts of the face are named.

TURN off the tape recorder and engage your child in the suggested activities for the day.

The sequence may take 5 to 20 minutes depending on the age of the learner and how much activity you choose to do.

Then, turn the tape recorder back on to hear the recorded lesson again.

Reinforce the lessons with the blue cassette at home or in the car, and at night before going to sleep.

How Often?

Try to have your OptimaLearning® language sessions once a day at about the same time. Repeat a lesson several times before going on to the next lesson. Then review it 3 or 4 days later, and at least twice during the following week. You are not trying to achieve mastery, just exposure, the first time through the course.

You're now ready to progress to the next level, or you can begin this cycle again, depending upon your child and how much French he or she is able to speak at this time. If your child is not yet speaking French or speaking very little, the continued review will be extremely beneficial.

If your child has memorized all the songs and dialogues and has begun to respond verbally to questions, keep using the language by reviewing and expanding activities. Listen to the tapes and dialogues as old family friends and favorite stories. Children love repetition, especially when they can actively participate in singing or telling the story.

The OptimaLearning® sequence should be followed for each lesson. Depending on your child's attention span, you may extend periods of play and improvisation, but always quit before your child is tired or bored.

Easy Does It !!

Above all, just as you wouldn't push your child, don't push yourself. The procedures in this workbook are designed for optimal results, but you may skip some of them if you don't feel motivated to do it all. OptimaLearning should be fun for both your child *and you*.

Listening is the first step in learning a language. Help your child become an active listener by showing your excitement and interest in the songs and dialogues. Let your face register emotion – wonderment, surprise, delight. As soon as possible, join in singing the songs as you learn them. Encourage your child to sing as well. As soon as a song is learned, sing it anywhere during the day, at home, and play the blue cassette (songs only) in the car. An ideal time for absorption and retention is in the so-called "twilight zone," in bed just before going to sleep, and right after waking.

Response to language is the next step in a child's learning. According to James Asher (author of *Total Physical Response*), you should let your child become physically involved before seeking verbal responses. For instance, point to the pictures, reach for the sun, enact the greeting process. The second lesson involves parts of the face. Have your child touch his or her face as the song is sung.

In the activities you can become as imaginative and playful as possible. Don't rush the child. Enjoy the absurd. Encourage laughter. Involving the total physical response is a key way we teach our children their native language, and it is especially effective for children learning a new language. Use the principles of OptimaLearning: acceptance, expectancy, rhythm and intonation, receptivity, and Educative Feedback.

Language learning for children and increased memory comes through repeated exposure from different angles and perspectives, according to research by Georgi Lozanov and Ivan Barzakov, and confirmed by studies of Karl Pribram, world-renowned neuroscientist, and Michael S. Gazzaniga, pioneering brain researcher and psychologist. Don't push your child to memorize – avoid struggle! Just continue to provide language exposure in regular, stress-free, playful environments.

We invite you to report your experiences to OptimaLearning Language Land™ (885 Olive Avenue, Suite A, Novato, CA 94945). We want to know how your child responded and what worked well for you.

Bon voyage!

PRONUNCIATION GUIDE

In French there are a certain number of accents on letters, such as grave (`), aigu/acute (´), circumflex (^), and cedilla (ç), which do not exist in English. We have listed and explained below how to pronounce French letters and sounds that include these symbols, which we have written after each French line of text. In our text you will find first a French phrase, a phonetic symbol phrase under it, and the English translation below that.

CONSONANTS

Letters	Pronunciation	Phonetic Symbol	Example
b, d, f, k, l, m,	as in English	b, d, f, k, l, m,	
n, p, t, v, x, z	as in English	n, p, t, v, x, z	
c (before e, y, i)	as 's' in sun	s	morceau (mohrso) *piece*
ç (before a, o, u)	as 's' in sun	s	garçon (gahrsohn̄g) *boy*
c (before a, o, u)	as 'k' in king	k	carte (kahrt) *menu or map*
ch	as 'sh' in shirt	sh	chéri (shayree) *darling*
g (before e, i, y)	as 's' in treasure	ž	manger (mahn̄gžay) *to eat*
g (before a, o, u)	as 'g' in garden	g	grand (grahn̄g) *big*
gn	as 'ni' in onion	n̲	mignon (meen̲on̄g) *cute*
h	never pronounced		haricot (ahreeko) *bean*
j	as 's' in pleasure	ž	jour (žoor) *day*
qu	as 'k' in key	k	queue (kuh) *line or tail*
q (only when final)	same as above	k	cinq (san̄gk) *five*
r	rolled in back of mouth like a soft gargle	r	rien (ryan̄g) *nothing*
s	as English 's'	s	sucre (sëwkr) *sugar*
s (between 2 vowels)	as 'z' in zoo	z	oiseau (wahzo) *bird*
th	as 't' in Tom	t	thé (tay) *tea*
w	as 'v' in Victor	v	wagon (vahgon̄g) *coach*

LIAISON

One of the reasons that the French language sounds so beautiful and so flowing is due to the liaison. The word liaison means 'linking' or 'connection'. Usually the final consonant is not pronounced in French. However, sometimes when a word ending in a consonant is followed by a vowel, the consonant *is* pronounced, as if it starts the next word.

Example: bon appetit   *bohn̄g-n-ahpehtee*   eat well

STRESS

In general, French syllables have more or less the same degree of stress (loudness), quite unlike English. Native French speakers can hear a slightly heavier stress on the last syllable of a word group, but this is not important for our purposes. Bear in mind that each syllable should be pronounced with equal stress.

VOWELS

Letters	Pronunciation	Phonetic Symbol	Example
a, à, â	as 'a' in father (but shorter)	ah	papa (pahpah) *daddy*
ai	as 'e' in eight	ay	j'ai (žay) *I have*
	or, as 'e' in best	eh	plaisir (plehzeer) *pleasure*
ail, aille	as 'igh' in high	igh	paille (pigh) *straw*
au, eau	as 'o' in no	o	beau (bo) *beautiful or handsome*
é, er, ez, ay	as 'e' in eight but as short vowel; no dipthong; 'e' not ei	ay	été (aytay) *summer*
è, ê, e, ei	as 'e' in best (but longer)	eh	mère (mehr) *mother*
e	as in unstressed 'e' in the	uh	le (luh) *the*
eil, eille	as in may	aye	oreille (ohraye) *ear*
eu, oeu	approximately like the unstressed 'e' in the	uh	feu (fuh) *fire* oeuf (uhf) *egg*
i, î	as 'ee' in meet (but shorter)	ee	il (eel) *he*
ille	as 'ee' in see (but with a soft 'yuh' added at end of word)	eë	fille (feë) *girl or daughter*
o, ô	generally like 'o' in oh sometimes like 'o' in no	oh o	porte (pohrt) *door* rose (roz) *rose*
oi, oî	as 'wa' in wa-wa (baby's expression for water)	wah	moi (mwah) *me* boîte (bwaht) *box*
ou, oû	as 'oo' in cool	oo	poupée (poopay) *doll*
u, û	something like 'ew' in stew (but with round protruded lips)	ëw	tu (tëw) *you [familiar form]*
ui	as 'wee' in week (but shorter) or as in Hughey (diminutive of the name Hugh)	wee ëwee	oui (wee) *yes* nuit (nëwee) *night*

NASAL SOUNDS

The major difference between the French and English languages involves the nasal quality of certain French sounds. Nasal sounds usually occur when 'n' or 'm' follow a vowel in the same syllable. Nasal sounds are produced through the mouth and the nose at the same time. The tip of the tongue never touches the roof of the mouth. In the text, sounds that are nasalized have 'n̄g' right after them—that is, 'bon' is pronounced as *'bohn̄g.'*

The following letter combinations represent the nasal sounds in French:

Letters	Pronunciation	Phonetic Symbol	Example
am, an, em, en	similar to 'arn' in barn	ahn̄g	maman (mamahn̄g) *mommy*
im, in, aim, ain	similar to 'ang' in rang	an̄g	faim (fan̄g) *hungry* main (man̄g) *hand*
ien	similar to 'yan' in Yankee	an̄g	bien (byan̄g) *well, good*
on, om	similar to 'ong' in song	ohn̄g	bon (bohn̄g) *good* ombre (ohn̄gbruh) *shadow*
um, un	about like 'un' in under, but with a greater resonance	uhn̄g	un (uhn̄g) *one or a*

BONJOUR
bohn̄ḡzoor
Hello

Bonjour tous les amis
bohn̄ḡzoor too lay-z-ahmee
Hello   all (my) friends

Bonjour, bonjour, bonjour

Bonjour le soleil, dans le ciel
bohn̄ḡzoor luh solaye, dahn̄ḡ luh syehl
Hello   sun,   in   the sky

Bonjour la terre, et l'univers.
bohn̄ḡzoor lah tehr, eh lëwneevehr.
Hello   earth, and the universe.

Bonjour Maman, ô ma maman
bohn̄ḡzoor mahmahn̄ḡ, oh mah mahmahn̄ḡ
Hello   Mama,   oh my Mama

Bonjour Maman, que j'aime tant.
bohn̄ḡzoor mahmahn̄ḡ, kuh žaym tahn̄ḡ.
Hello   Mama,   whom I love so much.

Bonjour Papa, ô mon papa
bohn̄ḡzoor pahpah, oh mohn̄ḡ pahpah
Hello   Daddy, oh my Daddy

Prends moi, Papa, entre tes bras.
prahn̄ḡ mwah, pahpah, ahn̄gtr tay brah.
Take me, Daddy, in your arms.

Bonjour tous les amis
bohn̄ḡzoor too lay-z-ahmee
Hello   all (my) friends

Bonjour, bonjour, bonjour

DIALOGUE

Christiane:

Bonjour, comment tu t'appelles?
bohn̄ḡzoor, kohmahn̄ḡ tëw tahpehl?
Hello,   what's   your name?

Bonjour, Nicolas.
bohn̄ḡzoor Neekolah.
Hello,   Nicolas.

Moi, je m'appelle, Christiane.
Mwah, žuh mahpehl Kreestyahn.
Me, I'm Christiane.

Qu'est-ce que c'est?
Kehskuhseh?
What is it?

Ah, un clown. Il est beau ton clown.
ah uhn̄ḡ kloon. eel eh bo tohn̄ḡ kloon.
Oh, a clown. He's beautiful, your clown.

Comment tu t'appelles, Clown?
kohmahn̄ḡ tëw tahpehl, kloon?
What's   your name, Clown?

Jojo?
žožo?
Jojo?

Regarde, Nicolas.
ruhgahrd, Neekolah.
Look,   Nicolas.

C'est ma guitare! Ecoute!
seh mah geetahr! ehkoot!
It's my guitar! Listen!

Nicolas:

Je m'appelle, Nicolas.
žuh mahpehl Neekolah.
My name is Nicolas.

Et toi, comment tu t'appelles?
eh twah, kohmahn̄ḡ tëw tahpehl?
And (you), what's your name?

Regarde, Christiane.
ruhgahrd, Kreestyahn.
Look,   Christiane.

C'est mon clown.
seh mohn̄ḡ kloon.
This is my clown.

Je m'appelle, Jojo.
žuh mahpehl, žožo.
My name is Jojo.

Oui, Jojo, Jojo le clown.
wee, žožo, žožo luh kloon.
Yes, Jojo, Jojo the clown.

Qu'est-ce que c'est?
kehskuhseh?
What is it?

VOCABULARY

qu'est-ce que c'est?
kehskuhseh?
What is this?

comment tu t'appelles?
kohmahn̄ḡ tëw tahpehl?
What's your name?

je m'appelle
žuh mahpehl
My name is

je t'aime —*žuh taym* —I love you

tes amis
tay-z-ahmee
your friends

c'est beau
seh bo
it's beautiful

regarde!
ruhgahrd!
Look!

ACTIVITIES

- Point to objects in picture to accompany song (sun, earth, sky, etc.).
- Repeat "Comment tu t'appelles" (what's your name) and find objects to name.
- Say "Comment tu t'appelles" and child answers "Je m'appelle" with his/her name.
- Hold up objects and say "Qu'est-ce que c'est?" and have child respond "C'est..." with name of the object.

Optional object: toy clown

8

CLOWN
kloon
Clown

Clown, Clown, Clown
kloon, kloon, kloon
Clown, clown, clown

Passe devant   la glace
pahs duhvahng lah glahs
Passes in front of the mirror

Il   fait des grimaces
eel feh day greemahs
He makes faces

Avec   le nez, le nez
ahvehk luh nay, luh nay
With (his) nose, (his) nose

Clown, Clown, Clown…

Avec   la bouche, la bouche
ahvehk lah boosh, lah boosh
With (his) mouth, (his) mouth

Le nez, le nez
luh nay, luh nay
(His) nose, (his) nose

Clown, Clown, Clown

Passe   devant   la glace
pahs   duhvahng lah glahs
Passes in front of the mirror

Il   fait des grimaces
eel feh day greemahs
He makes faces

Avec   les yeux, la bouche,   le nez
ahvehk lay-z-yuh, lah boosh,   luh nay
With   (his) eyes, (his) mouth, (his) nose

Clown, Clown, Clown…

Avec   les oreilles, les oreilles
ahvehk lay-z-oraye, lay-z-oraye
With   (his) ears, (his) ears

Clown, Clown, Clown…

Avec les joues, les oreilles, les yeux, la bouche, le nez
ahvehk lay žoo…
With the cheeks…(repeat parts of face)

Clown, Clown, Clown…

Avec le menton, les joues, les oreilles, les yeux, la bouche, le nez
ahvehk luh mahngtohng…
With the chin…

Clown, Clown, Clown…

Plus vite!
plëw veet!
Faster!

Avec les cheveux, le menton, les joues, les oreilles, les yeux, la bouche, le nez
ahvehk lay shuhvuh, luh mahngtohng…
With (his) hair…

DIALOGUE

Attention, oh là là, tu vas tomber
ahtahngsyohng, oh lah lah, tëw vah tohngbay
Watch out, you're going to fall

Patatras! Devant la glace
          duhvahng lah glahs
(Crash!)   in front of the mirror

Lève-toi, Clown
lehv twah, kloon
Get up, Clown

Voilà!
vwahlah!
There we go!

(Song repeats)

VOCABULARY

la glace	il fait des grimaces
lah glahs	*eel feh day greemahs*
the mirror	he makes faces
avec	lève-toi
ahvehk	*lehv twah*
with	get up
devant	attention
duhvahng	*ahtahngsyohng*
in front of	watch out
voilà	
vwahlah	
There you go	

ACTIVITIES

- Child points to parts of face as sung in song and shown in picture.
- Pretend to be clowns and make faces and fall in front of the mirror.
- Use "Qu'est-ce que c'est" (*kehskuh-seh*) [what is this] for parts of face.
- Parent or adult uses expression "lève-toi" (*lehv twah*) [get up] when appropriate.
- Use game of Simon Says to reinforce parts of face.

Optional object: toy clown

LE CHAT
luh shah
The cat

Chat chat chat, chat chat chat,
chat couché dans son panier.
shah shah shah, shah shah shah,
shah kooshay dahng sohng pahnyay.
Cat cat cat, cat cat cat,
cat sleeping in his basket.

Chat chat chat, chat chat chat,
chat couché bien au chaud.
shah shah shah, shah shah shah,
shah kooshay byang o sho.
Cat cat cat, cat cat cat,
cat sleeping nice and warm.

Chien chien chien, chien chien chien,
chien couché dans sa niche.
shyang shyang shyang, shyang shyang shyang,
shyang kooshay dahng sah neesh.
Dog dog dog, dog dog dog,
dog sleeping in his house.

Chien chien chien, chien chien chien,
chien couché bien au chaud.
shyang shyang shyang, shyang shyang shyang ,
shyang kooshay byang o sho.
Dog dog dog, dog dog dog,
dog sleeping nice and warm.

DIALOGUE

Christiane:

Miaou, miaou, miaou
myahoo myahoo, myahoo
meow, meow, meow

Qui est là?
kee eh lah
Who is there?

Il est beau.
eel eh bo
He is beautiful

Miaou!
Myahoo!
Meow!

Nicolas:

Minet minet, viens, viens.
meeneh meeneh, vyang, vyang.
Kitty kitty, come, come.

C'est mon chat. Viens voir.
seh mohng shah. vyang vwahr.
It's my cat. Come here.

Oui, regarde sa queue, ses moustaches.
wee, ruhgahrd sah kuh, say moostahsh.
Yes, look at his tail, his whiskers.

Attention, Christiane!
ahtahngsyohng, Kreestyahn!
Watch out, Christiane!

Caresse le. Il est doux!
kahrehs luh. eel eh doo!
Pet him. He's soft!

VOCABULARY

viens! *vyang*	come!
qui est là? *kee eh lah?*	who is there?
caresse-le! *kahrehs luh!*	pet him!
le chat *luh shah*	the cat
le chien *luh shyang*	the dog
il est beau *ee-l-eh bo*	he is beautiful
regarde! *ruhgahrd*	look!
attention! *ahtahngsyohng*	watch out!
chaud *sho*	hot, warm
froid *frwah*	cold
viens voir! *vyang vwahr!*	come see!
viens ici! *vyang-z-eesee!*	come here!

ACTIVITIES

- Point out things in the picture that correspond with the song, using:
  "Qu'est-ce que c'est?" *kehskuhseh* "What is this?" and "C'est" *seh* "It is"
- Pretend to be a sleeping cat or dog.
- Act out the scene in the dialogue.
  Optional objects: stuffed cat or dog.

12

LA FÊTE DES CANARDS
lah feht day kahnahr
The Ducks' Party

C'est la fête des canards,
  dans la mare, dans la mare
seh lah feht day kahnahr,
  dahng lah mahr, dahng lah mahr,
It's the duck's party,
  in the marsh, in the marsh

C'est la fête des canards,
  coin, coin, coin, coin, coin
Seh lah feht day kahnahr,
  kwehng, kwehng, kwehng, kwehng, kwehng
It's the duck's party,
  quack, quack, quack, quack, quack

Les oiseaux battent de l'aile
lay-z-wahzo baht duh lehl
The birds flap their wings

Dans le ciel, dans le ciel, les oiseaux...
  cui, cui, cui, cui, cui
dahng luh syehl, dahng luh syehl, lay-z-wahzo...
  kwee, kwee, kwee, kwee, kwee
In the sky, in the sky, the birds...
  tweet, tweet, tweet, tweet, tweet

Les poules viennent à la fête
lay pool vyehn ah lah feht
The hens come to the party

Cot codette, elles caquettent, les poules...
kot kodeht, ehl kahkeht, lay pool...
Cluck cluck, they are cackling, the hens...

Puis le coq est arrivé
Pëwee luh kohk eh-t-ahreevay
Then the rooster came in

Sans se presser, sans se presser
sahng suh prehsay, sahng suh prehsay
Taking his time, taking his time

Puis le coq est arrivé
Pëwee luh kohk eh-t-ahreevay
Then the rooster came in

Co co co rico, co co rico
Ko ko reeko, ko ko reeko
Cock a doodle doo, cock a doodle doo

DIALOGUE

Christiane:
Nicolas, on joue à "Qu'est-ce que c'est?"
Nikolah, ohng žoo ah kehskuhseh?
Nicolas, let's play at "What is this?"

Nicolas:
D'accord.
dahkohr.
Okay.

Christiane:
Alors, vas-y.
ahlohr, vah-z-ee.
Well, go ahead.

C'est la vache.
Seh lah vahsh.
It's the cow.

Nicolas:
Qu'est-ce que c'est? Meu meu.
Kehskuhseh? Muh muh.
What is this? Moo moo.

Oui, c'est bien.
Wee seh byang.
Yes, that's it.

Christiane:
C'est le chat.
seh luh shah.
It's cat.

Nicolas:
Qu'est-ce que c'est? Miaou, miaou.
Kehskuhseh? myahoo, myahoo.
What is this? Meow, meow.

Oui, c'est bon.
Wee, seh bohng.
Yes, that's good.

Christiane:
Cot cot codette?
C'est le coq.
seh luh kohk.
It's the rooster.

Nicolas:
Qu'est-ce que c'est? Cot cot codette.
Kehskuhseh? kot kot kodeht.
What is this? Cluck, cluck, cluck.

Non, ce n'est pas le coq. C'est la poule.
nohng, suh neh pah luh kohk. seh lah pool.
No, it's not the rooster. It's the hen.

Le coq fait co co rico.
luh kohk fay ko ko reeko.
The rooster does cock a doodle do.

Christiane:
Maintenant tu fais le coq.
mangtuhnahng tëw fay luh kohk.
Now you do the rooster.

Je fais la vache et voici le canard.
žuh fay lah vahsh eh vwahsee luh kahnahr.
I'll do the cow and here is the duck.

(See page 30 for Activities
and Vocabulary)

14

FLIC FLOC
fleek flohk
Splish Splash

Prends ton parapluie, ma mie.
prahng tohng pahrahplëwee, mah mee.
Take your umbrella, my friend.

Prends ton parapluie, ma mie.
prahng tohng pahrahplëwee, mah mee.
Take your umbrella, my friend.

Il pleut, il mouille.
eel pluh, eel mooyeë
It is raining, it is wet (outside).

Prends ton parapluie, ma mie.
prahng tohng pahrahplëwee, mah mee.
Take your umbrella, my friend.

Flic floc, flic floc, flic, floc floc
fleek flohk, fleek flohk, fleek flohk flohk
Splish splash, splish splash, splish, splash splash

Flic floc, flic floc, dans les flaques d'eau.
fleek, flohk, fleek, flohk, dahng lay flahk do.
Splish, splash, splish, splash, in the puddles.

```
┌─────────────────────────────────────┐
│  ACTIVITIES                          │
│                                      │
│ • Point out objects in picture       │
│ • Act out song (pretend to walk      │
│   around puddles, make sound of      │
│   rain with fingertips)              │
│ • Play "C'est grand ou petit?"       │
│       seh grahng oo puhtee?          │
│       Is this big or little?         │
│   Child responds beginning with:     │
│       "C'est"                        │
│       seh                            │
│       It is                          │
│ • Play "C'est mouillé ou sec?"       │
│       seh mooyay oo sehk?            │
│       Is it wet or dry?              │
│    Again, child responds beginning   │
│    with:                             │
│       "C'est"                        │
│       seh                            │
│       It is                          │
│ • Sing "Flic floc" in the bathtub    │
│   using words wet, dry, frog,        │
│   rain, etc.                         │
│                                      │
│ Optional Objects: Umbrella, toy frog │
└─────────────────────────────────────┘
```

DIALOGUE

Christiane and Nicolas:

Il pleut, il mouille
eel pluh, eel mooyeë
It is raining, it is wet (outside)

C'est
seh
It is

C'est la
seh lah
It is the

C'est la fête
seh lah feht
It is the festival

A la
ah lah
Of the

A la grenouille!
ah lah gruhnooyeë!
Of the frog!

Il pleut il mouille c'est la fête à la grenouille.
eel pluh eel mooyeë seh lah feh-t-ah lah gruhnooyeë
It is raining, it is wet (outside), it is the festival of the frog.

```
┌─────────────────────────────────────┐
│  VOCABULARY                          │
│                                      │
│  prends!            c'est            │
│  prahng             seh              │
│  take!              it is            │
│                                      │
│  le parapluie       mouillé          │
│  luh pahrahplëwee   mooyay           │
│  the umbrella       wet              │
│                                      │
│  il pleut           grand            │
│  eel pluh           grahng           │
│  It is raining      big              │
│                                      │
│  la grenouille      petit            │
│  lah gruhnooyeë     puhtee           │
│  the frog           little           │
│                                      │
│  la fête                             │
│  lah feht                            │
│  the festival                        │
└─────────────────────────────────────┘
```

POLICHINELLE
poleesheenehl
Jumping Jack

Je   tire sur la ficelle Poli Polichinelle
žuh teer sëwr lah feesehl polee poleesheenehl
I   pull on   the string, Jumping Jack

Je   tire sur la ficelle, Polichinelle se réveille!
žuh teer sëwr lah feesehl poleesheenehl suh rehvaye!
I pull on the string, the Jumping Jack wakes up!

Hop et hop et ah!

Ses mains sont en haut
say ma̅ng sohng-t-ahng o
His hands are up high

Hop et hop et ah!

Ses mains sont en bas
say ma̅ng sohng-t-ahng bah
His hands are   down

P'tit tourbillon,   grand tourbillon
p'tee toorbeeyohng, grahng toorbeeyohng
Little whirlwind,   big   whirlwind

Hop et hop et ah! Hop et hop et ah!

Ses bras sont en   haut, ses bras sont en   bas
say brah sohng-t-ahng o, say brah sohng-t-ahng bah
His arms are   up, his arms are   down

Ses pieds sont en   haut, ses pieds sont en   bas
say pyeh sohng-t-ahng o, say pyeh sohng-t-ahng bah
His feet are   up, his feet are   down

Ses jambes sont en   haut, ses jambes sont en   bas
say žahngb sohng-t-ahng o, say žahngb sohng-t-ahng bah
His legs are   up, his legs are   down

Sa tête est en   haut, sa tête est en   bas
sah teht eh-t-ahng o,   sah teht eh-t-ahng bah
His head is   up, his head is   down

P'tit tourbillon, grand tourbillon
p'tee toorbeeyohng, grahng toorbeeyohng
Little whirlwind, big whirlwind

Hop et hop et ah!
Hop et hop et ah!

ACTIVITIES

- Pantomine pulling string, waking up
- Act out song (arms up and down, legs up and down, etc.)
- Use <u>Simon Says</u> to reinforce learning names of body parts, using "en haut" *(ahng o)* [up] and "en bas" *(ahng bah)* [down].
- Play "Moulin" *(moolang)* [windmill] using appropriate gestures and saying "Grand tourbillon" *(grahng toorbeeohng)* [big whirlwind] and "Petit tourbillon" *(p'tee toorbeeyohng)* [little whirlwind].

Optional object: Jumping Jack

DIALOGUE

Frappe des mains
frahp day ma̅ng
Clap hands

Touche tes bras. Bravo!
toosh tay brah. brahvo!
Touch your arms. Bravo!

Tape des pieds
tahp day pyeh
Tap (your) feet

Touche tes jambes. Bravo!
toosh tay žahngb. brahvo!
Touch your legs. Bravo!

Frappe des mains
frahp day ma̅ng
Clap hands

Et tape des pieds. Bravo!
eh tahp day pyeh. brahvo!
And tap your feet. Bravo!

Tourne la tête
toorn lah teht
Turn (your) head

Tête en haut
teh-t-ahng o
Head up high

Tête en bas. Bravo!
teh-t-ahng bah. brahvo!
Head down low. Bravo!

Tourne les mains
toorn lay ma̅ng
Turn (your) hands

P'tit moulin, p'tit moulin
p'tee moolang, p'tee moolang
Little windmill, little windmill

P'tit tourbillon,   p'tit tourbillon,   bravo!
p'tee toorbeeyohng, p'tee toorbeeyohng, brahvo!
Little whirlwind,   little whirlwind,   bravo!

Tourne, tourne
toorn, toorn
Turn, turn

Grand moulin, grand tourbillon, bravo!
grahng moolang, grahng toorbeeyohng, brahvo!
Big windmill, big whirlwind, bravo!

Et saute, saute saute sauterelle!
eh sot, sot sot   sotrehl!
And jump, jump, jump grasshopper!

VOCABULARY

réveille-toi
rayvaye twah
wake-up

ne frappe pas
nuh frahp pah
don't hit

ne tape pas
nuh tahp pah
don't tap

ne touche pas
nuh toosh pah
don't touch

petit
puhtee
small, little

grand
grahng
big

tout petit
too p'tee
so small

très grand
treh grahng
very big

c'est petit
seh p'tee
it's small

c'est grand
seh grahng
it's big

"où est"
oo eh
where is

"regarde"
ruhgahrd
look

"Qu'est-ce que c'est?"
kehskuhseh
What is this?

18

PAPILLON

Butterfly

Papillon   vole, vole
pahpeeyohng vohl vohl
Butterfly,   fly,   fly

Papillon   dans   la   fleur
pahpeeyohng dahng lah fluhr
Butterfly,   in   the flower

Papillon   vole, vole
pahpeeyohng vohl vohl
Butterfly,   fly,   fly

Papillon   sur   mon   coeur
pahpeeyohng sëwr mohng kuhr
Butterfly   on   my   heart

(Refrain repeats)

DIALOGUE

Christiane:
Nicolas, où es tu?
neekolah, oo eh tëw
Nicolas, where are you?

Vole vole papillon!
vohl vohl pahpeeyohng!
Fly, fly butterfly!

Dis moi où est ta maison?
dee mwah oo eh tah mayzohng
Tell me, where is your house?

Vole vole papillon!

Dis moi,   où vas tu   jouer, polisson?
dee mwah, oo vah tëw žooay, pohleesohng
Tell me, where do you go to play, little rascal?

Vole vole papillon!

Dis moi, qui sont tes amis, tes compagnons?
dee mwah kee sohng tay-z-ahmee, tay kohngpahnohng
Tell me, who are your friends, your playmates?

Et qui encore?
eh kee ahngkohr?
And who else?

Nicolas:
Chut!   Je   suis   un   papillon.
shëwt! žuh sëwee uhng pahpeeyohng
Shhh!   I'm   a   butterfly.

Dans l'arbre.
dahng lahrbr
In the tree.

Dans les fleurs.
dahng lay fluhr
In the flowers.

La mouche!
lah moosh
The fly!

L'abeille!
lahbaye!
The bee!

ACTIVITIES

- Make a picture of butterfly wings with a child, and cut them out to use with the song.
- Children, as they listen to the song, fly like butterflies; pretend to be small flowers.
- Pantomine song, being a bee, fly, flower.
- Point to picture and use French words to identify bee, fly, tree, flower, butterfly.
- On nature walks, use French forms for flower, bee, etc.

Optional Object: butterfly wings

VOCABULARY

mon coeur *mohng kuhr** my heart	dans l'arbre *dahng lahrbr* in the tree	
ton coeur *tohng kuhr** your heart	les fleurs *lay fluhr* the flowers	
où es-tu? *oo eh tëw* where are you?	la maison *lah mayzohng* the house	
dis-moi! *dee mwah* tell me!	encore! *ahngkohr!* again!	
	qui encore? *kee-ahngkohr?* who else?	

*term of endearment

20

AU MARCHÉ
o mahrshay
At the Open Air Market

Au marché   de   l'Opéra
o mahrshay duh lopayrah
At the market of the Opera *

J'ai acheté   un,   un   ananas.
žay ahshuhtay uhn̄g, uhn̄g-n-anahnah
I   bought   one, one pineapple.

Et puis encore?   Des avocats.
eh pëwee-z-ahn̄gkohr? day-z-ahvokah
And then what else?   Some avocados.

Au marché de la rue Mouffetard
o marshay duh lah rëw mooftahr
At the market of Mouffetard Street

J'ai acheté   un, deux, deux poires.
žay ahshuhtay uhn̄g, duh, duh pwahr
I   bought   one, two, two pears.

Et puis encore?   Des épinards.
eh pëwee-z-ahn̄gkohr? day-z-aypeenahr
And then what else?   Some spinach.

Au marché du Bois de Boulogne...
o mahrshay dëw bwah duh boolohn
At the market of the Woods of Boulogne...

Un, deux, trois, trois pommes.
uhn̄g, duh, trwah, trwah pohm
One, two, three, three apples.

Et puis encore?   Des pommes de terre.
eh pëwee-z-ahn̄gkohr? day pohm duh tehr
And then what else?   Some   potatoes.

Au marché du Père Lachaise...
o mahrshay dëw pehr la shehz
At the market of Father LaChaise...

Un, deux, trois, quatre,   quatre fraises.
uhn̄g, duh, trwah, kahtr,   kahtr frehz.
One, two, three, four,   four strawberries.

Et puis encore?   Des cacahuètes.
eh pëwee-z-ahn̄gkohr? day kahkahweht
And then what else?   Some peanuts.

Au marché du Trocadéro...
o mahrshay dëw trokahdayro
At the market of Trocadero...

J'ai acheté   un, deux, trois, quatre, cinq,
   cinq artichauts.
*žay ahshuhtay uhn̄g, duh, trwah, kahtr, san̄gk,
   san̄gk ahrteesho*
I   bought   one, two, three, four,   five,
   five artichokes.

Et puis encore?   Des abricots.
eh pëwee-z-ahn̄gkohr? day-z-abreeko
And then what else?   Some apricots.

VOCABULARY

donne-moi!
don mwah
give me!

devine!
duhveen
guess

quoi?
kwah
what?

bien
byan̄g
well

c'est bon
say bohn̄g
it's good

j'en voudrais
žahn̄g voodreh
I would like some

j'ai acheté
žay ahshuhtay
I bought

et puis encore?
eh pëwee-z-ahn̄gkohr?
and then what else?

encore
ahn̄gkohr
more

est-ce que tu en veux encore?
ehskuh tëw ahn̄g vuh ahn̄gkohr?
do you want some more?

---

*The expression *traderi traderi dera* and several rhythm variations of this phrase are repeated throughout this song. They simply mean la di da da di da, or tra la la la la.

22

Au marché de la gare de Lyon...
o mahrshay duh lah gahr duh leeohng
At the market of the Lyon train station...

Un, deux, trois, quatre, cinq, six, six
 champignons.
*uhng, duh, trwah, kahtr, sangk, sees, see
 shahngpeenohng*
One, two, three, four, five, six, six mushrooms.

Et puis encore? Du poisson.
eh pëwee-z-ahngkohr? dëw pwahsohng.
And then what else? Some fish.

Au marché de Montmartre...
o mahrshay duh mohngmahrtr
At the market of Montmartre...

Un, deux, trois, quatre, cinq, six, sept, sept
 tomates.
*uhng, duh, trwah, kahtr, sangk, sees, seht, seht
 tomaht*
One, two, three, four, five, six, seven, seven tomatoes.

Et puis encore? Des aromates.
eh pëwee-z-ahngkohr? day-z-ahromaht
And then what else? Some herbs.

Au marché de la Bastille...
o mahrshay duh lah bahsteë
At the market of the Bastille...

Un, deux, trois, quatre, cinq, six, sept, huit,
 huit radis.
*uhng, duh, trwah, kahtr, sangk, sees, seht, ëweet,
 ëwee rahdee*
One, two, three, four, five, six, seven, eight,
 eight radishes.

Et puis encore? Du persil.
eh pëwee-z-ahngkohr? dëw pehrseel
And then what else? Some parsley.

Au marché de l'Orangerie...
o mahrshay duh lohrahngžuhree
At the market of the Orangerie...

Un, deux, trois, quatre, cinq, six, sept, huit,
 neuf, neuf oranges.
*uhng, duh, trwah, kahtr, sangk, sees, seht, ëweet,
 nuhf, nuhf orahngž*
One, two, three, four, five, six, seven, eight,
 nine, nine oranges.

Et puis encore? Du fromage.
eh pëwee-z-ahngkohr? dëw fromahž
And then what else? Some cheese.

Au marché de Pampelune...
o mahrshay duh pahngplëwn
At the market of Pampelune...

Un, deux, trois, quatre, cinq, six, sept, huit,
 neuf, dix, dix prunes.
*uhng, duh, trwah, kahtr, sangk, sees, seht, ëweet,
 nuhf, dees, dee prëwn*
One, two, three, four, five, six, seven, eight,
 nine, ten, ten plums.

Et puis encore?
eh pëwee-z-ahngkohr?
And then what else?

Devine?
duhveen
Guess?

Quoi?
kwah
What?

Et bien?
eh byang
And well?

Dis moi.
dee mwah
Tell me.

La lune!
lah lëwn!
The moon!

ACTIVITIES

- Reinforce the numbers and use
 expression "Combien?"
 (kohnbyang) ["How much?"]
- Point to fruit and vegetables in
 picture and around the house
 and use expression "Qu'est-ce
 que c'est?" *(kehskuhseh)*
 ["What is this?"]
- Encourage child to move with the
 music.
- As child puts a vegetable or fruit
 in basket, he or she names it.
 Have child give fruit or vegetable
 to adult while using expression.
- Make cut-outs of vegetables and
 fruits.
- When going to the market, use it
 as a place to practice words.

Objects: Basket with real or plastic
fruits and vegetables.

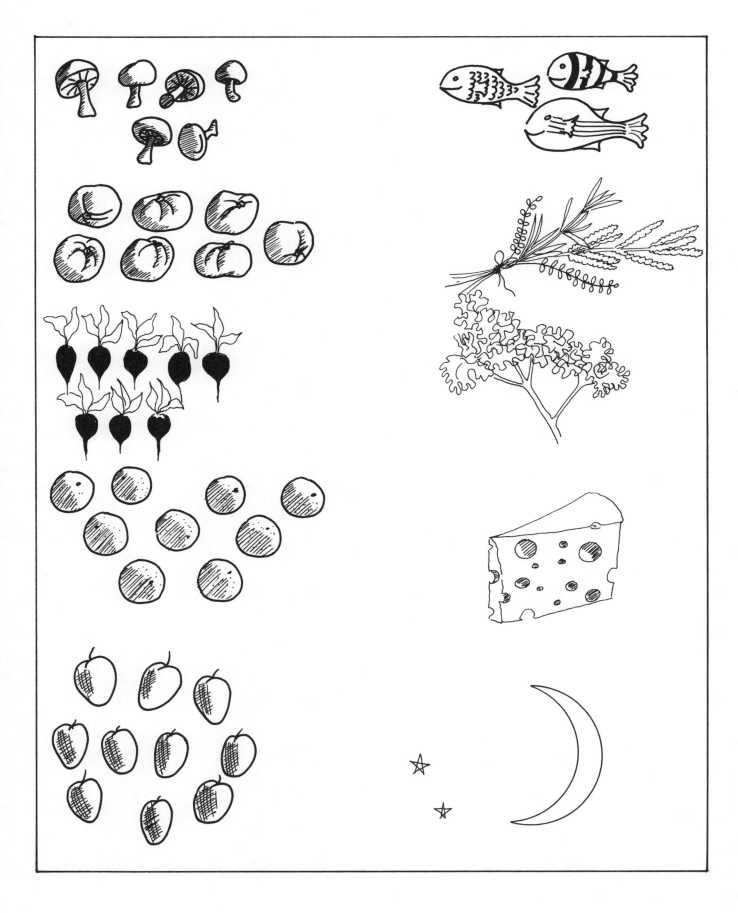

BON APPÉTIT
bohng-n-ahpaytee
Eat well (Good appetite)

Miam(e), miam(e), miam(e), miam(e), miam(e)!
meeyahmuh, meeyahmuh...
Yummy, yummy, yummy, yummy!

J'ai faim, j'ai faim!
žay fang, žay fang
I'm hungry, I'm hungry!

Maman, maman
mahmahng, mahmahng
Mommy, Mommy

Comment? Comment? Que veux-tu,
mon enfant?
*kohmahng? kohmahng? Kuh vuh tëw,
monhng-n-ahngfahng?*
What? What is it? What do you want,
my child?

Maman, maman, je voudrais bien...
mahmahng, mahmahng, žuh voodreh byang...
Mommy, Mommy, I would like...

Je voudrais, s'il vous plaît*
žuh voodreh, seel voo play
I would like, please

Je voudrais, s'il vous plaît

Un oeuf à la coque
uhng-n-uhf ah lah kohk
A soft boiled egg

Avec une tartine
ahveh-k-ëwn tahrteen
With a piece of bread and butter

Des pâtes, de la salade, du fromage,
day paht, duh lah sahlahd, dëw fromahž;
Some noodles, some salad, some cheese,

Un yaourt; et surtout, un gâteau.
uhng yahoort; eh sëwrtoo, uhng gahto
A yogurt; and especially, a (piece of) cake.

*You may also say: s'il te plaît

Oh le gourmand!
o luh goormahng!
Oh, what a gourmand!

Miam(e), miam(e), miam(e), miam(e)...
meeyahmuh, meeyahmuh...
Yummy, yummy, yummy, yummy...

C'est bon, c'est bon!
seh bohng, seh bohng!
It's good, it's good!

Maman, maman
mahmahng, mahmahng
Mommy, Mommy

Comment? Comment? Que veux-tu,
mon enfant?
*kohmahng? kohmahng? Kuh vuh tëw,
mohng-n-ahngfahng?*
What? What? What do you want,
my child?

Merci, merci, cela suffit.
mehrsee, mehrsee, suhlah sëwfee.
Thank you, thank you, that's enough.

Mange bien, bon appétit.
mahngž byang, bohng-n-ahpaytee.
Eat well, good appetite.

Bon appétit.

VOCABULARY

j'ai faim	*žay fang*	I'm hungry
que veux-tu?	*kuh vuh tëw?*	What do you want?
je veux	*žuh vuh*	I want
surtout	*sëwrtoo*	especially
ça suffit	*sah sëwfee*	that's enough
ce n'est pas bon	*suh neh pah bohng*	that is not good
j'ai soif	*žay swahf*	I'm thirsty
je voudrais	*žuh voodreh?*	I would like
et	*eh*	and
cela suffit	*suhlah sëwfee*	that is enough
c'est bon	*seh bohng*	that's good
bon appétit!	*bohng-n-ahpaytee*	eat well

ACTIVITIES

- Feed a doll favorite food, using French words
- Use food in house to review vocabulary
- Adult encourages polite forms:
  merci / *mehrsee* / thank you
  s'il vous plaît / *seel voo play* / please
  s'il te plaît / *seel tuh play* / please (familiar)
- When asking a question, use "Comment?" (*kohmahng*) [what/how is it?]
- Using a drawing, ask the questions:
  "Qu'est-ce que c'est?" / *kehskuhseh?* / What is this?
  "Tu aimes ça?" / *tëw aym sah?* / Do you like that?
  Child answers: "C'est bon." / *seh bohng.* / That's good.

Optional objects: food from songs, doll

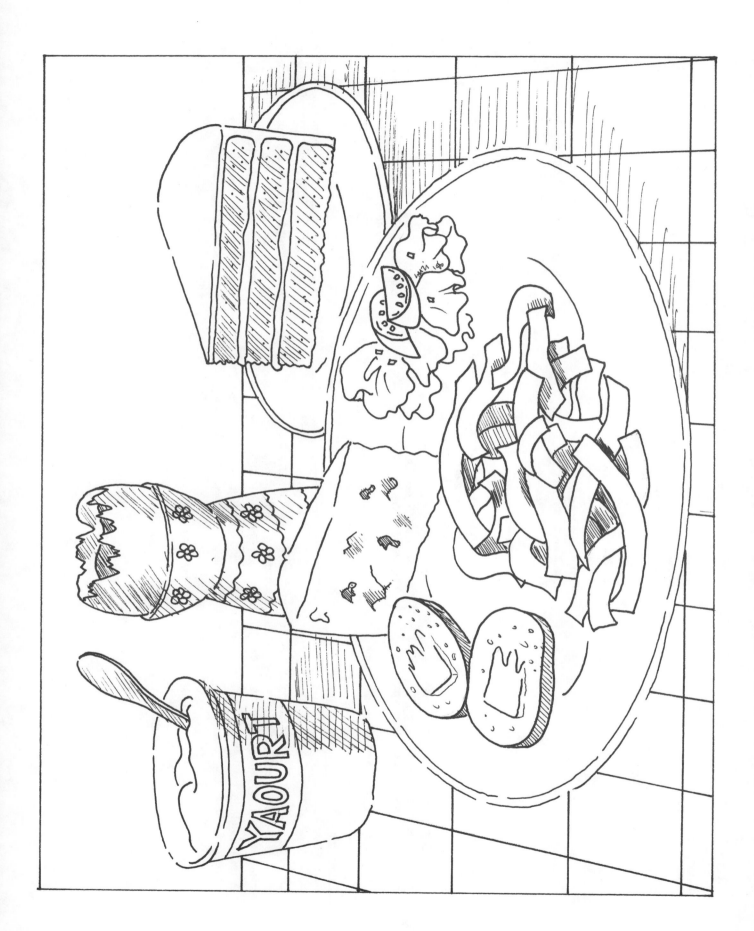

BONNE NUIT
bon-n-ëwee
Good Night

A pas de loup, soleil se couche
tout doux, tout doux.
*ah pah duh loo, solaye suh koosh
too doo, too doo.*
Creeping softly, the sun sets
softly, softly.

Il devient rouge. A pas de loup
soleil se couche.
*eel duhvyang rooż. ah pah duh loo
solaye suh koosh.*
It becomes red. Creeping softly,
the sun sets.

Tout doucement, il devient rouge.
too doosuhmahng, eel duhvyang rooż.
Quietly, it becomes red.

Do, do, do, do, petit!
do, do, do, do, do, puhtee!
byang o sho.
Bien au chaud.
Sleep, sleep, sleep, sleep, sleep, little one!
All warm and cuddly.

Dans ton lit.
dahng tohng lee.
In your bed.

Do, do, do, do, petit!
do, do, do, do, do, puhtee!
Sleep, sleep, sleep, sleep, little one!

A pas de loup, les étoiles brillent, tout doux, tout doux, (tout doucement) elles scintillent.
ah pah duh loo, lay-z-ehtwahl breë, too doo, too doo, (too doosuhmahng), ehl sahngteeë. they twinkle.
Creeping softly, the stars shine, softly, softly, (quietly)

A pas de loup, la lune se pose, tout doux, tout doux, (tout doucement) elle repose.
ah pah duh loo, lah lëwn suh poz, too doo, too doo, (too doosuhmahng), ehl ruhpoz.
Creeping softly, the moon sits down, softly, softly, (quietly) it rests.

Il faut dormir avec la nuit.
eel fo dohrmeer ahvehk lah nëwee.
You have to sleep with the night.

Christiane:

Nicolas, le soleil se couche.
Neekolah, luh solaye suh koosh.
Nicolas, the sun is setting.

C'est l'heure d'aller au lit.
seh luhr dahlay o lee.
It's time to go to bed.

Nicolas:

Déjà?
dayżah?
Already?

Où est mon pyjama?
oo eh mohng peeżahmah?
Where are my pajamas?

Christiane:

Oui, tout de suite.
wee, toot sweet.
Yes, right away.

Le voilà!
luh vwahlah.
Here they are!

Couche toi bien vite. Fais de beaux rêves.
koosh twah byang veet. feh duh bo rehv.
Get to sleep quickly. Have beautiful dreams.

Bonne nuit, Nicolas.
bon-n-ëwee, Neekolah.
Good night, Nicolas.

Nicolas:

Merci, Christiane, et toi aussi. Bonne nuit.
mehrsee, Kreestyahn, eh twah osee. bon-n-ëwee.
Thank you, Christiane, and you too. Good night.

Bonne nuit mon clown, bonne nuit
mon chat, mon chien.
*bon-n-ëwee mohng kloon, bon-n-ëwee
mohng shah, mon shyang.*
Good night my clown, good night
my cat, my dog.

Bonne nuit Maman, bonne nuit Papa.
bon-n-ëwee mahmahng, bon-n-ëwee, pahpah.
Good night, Mommy, good night, Daddy.

Bonne nuit la lune, bonne nuit les étoiles.
bon-n-ëwee lah lëwn, bon-n-ëwee lay-z-ehtwahl.
Good night the moon, good night the stars.

Bonne nuit tout le monde!!!
bon-n-ëwee too luh mohngd!!!
Good night everyone!!!

(See page 30 for Activities and Vocabulary)

LA FÊTE DES CANARDS

ACTIVITIES

- Adult makes animal noises, child repeats and then they switch.
- Adult may say:
  "Je fais la vache."
  žuh fay lah vahsh
  I am the cow.
  "Et tu fais le coq."
  eh tëw fay luh kohk.
  And you are the rooster.
- Use plastic farm animals as a way to use vocabulary.
- Reinforce vocabulary outside in a nature setting.

Optional objects: plastic farm animals, pictures of birds, ducks, etc.

VOCABULARY

la fête	*lah feht*	the party
le ciel	*luh syehl*	the sky
les poules	*lay pool*	the chickens (hens)
qu'est-ce que c'est?	*kehskuhseh*	what is this?
maintenant	*mangtuhmahng*	now
les canards	*lay kahnahr*	the ducks
les oiseaux	*lay-z-wahzo*	the birds
vas-y	*vah-z-ee*	go ahead
la vache	*lah vahsh*	the cow
comment fait?	*kohmahng fay?*	how you do this?

BONNE NUIT

VOCABULARY

les étoiles	*lay-z-aytwahl*	the stars
la lune	*la lëwn*	the moon
bonne nuit	*bon-n-ëwee*	good night
tout le monde	*too luh mohngd*	everyone
le pyjama	*luh peežahmah*	pajamas
le pullover	*luh pëwlohvehr*	the sweater
les pantoufles	*lay pahngtoofl*	slippers
les souliers	*lay sooleeeh*	the shoes
les chaussettes	*lay shoseht*	the socks
la chemise	*lah shuhmeez*	the shirt
lentement	*lahngtmahng*	slowly
vite	*veet*	quick/quickly

doux	*doo*	soft
dur	*dëwr*	hard
petit	*puhtee, p'tee*	little
moyen	*mwahyang*	medium
enlever	*ahngluhvay*	to take off
enlève!	*ahngluhv*	take off!
mettre	*mehtr*	to put on
mets!	*meh*	put on!
où est?	*oo eh?*	where is?
grand	*grahng*	big
couche-toi	*koosh twah*	go to bed
tout de suite	*toot sweet*	right away

ACTIVITIES

- Act out song
- While singing song, child uses a doll and puts it to sleep
- Play this song at night before bed as a ritual
- Point and guess what is *soft, hard, small, big and middle* size
- Say *good night* to Mommy, Daddy, familiar objects; to the moon and stars
- Practice with *where is* and *where are* with plural objects:

Examples:

Où est papa?	*oo eh pahpah?*	Il est ici.	*ee-l-eh-t-eesee.*	He is here.
Where is Daddy?				
Où est le clown?	*oo eh luh kloon?*	Il est là-bas.	*ee-l-eh lah bah.*	He is over there.
Where is the clown?				
Où est?	*oo eh*	where is		
Où sont?	*oo sohng*	where are		

Optional objects: familiar stuffed animals

SUPPLEMENTARY VOCABULARY

On Tape 1 Side 2 (red label) and on Tape 2 Side 2 (blue label) you will hear vocabulary words with a background of Baroque music. This music has been specially selected and the words are read with specific intonations to affect receptivity and long term memory.

Find a comfortable and quiet place to sit and relax for a few moments. Read along as you listen to the supplementary vocabulary words. Now, rewind the tape. This time, close the workbook and just enjoy the new vocabulary and the music. You may even want to close your eyes. The idea is to allow the information to slide into your memory without any conscious effort to memorize.

During the days that follow, listen to the same vocabulary several times. Be sure and pronounce the words out loud, closely following the speaker's intonation. To avoid monotony and vary the input of the new information into your memory system, use small gestures imitating a French person. Another time make larger movements with each word; on yet another occasion pretend you are an actor preparing an audition for the Comédie Française. Experiment with different pitches of voice as well.

If your child or children are in the vicinity, just allow the recording to play without drawing attention to it. You will be surprised to find how well children pick up words and phrases "peripherally."

Les Couleurs
Lay kooluhr
the colors

c'est bleu
say bluh
it's blue

c'est rouge
say roož
it's red

c'est jaune
say žon
it's yellow

c'est blanc, noir, orange, vert, brun
say blahng, nwahr, ohrahngž, vehr, bruhng
it's white, black, orange, green, brown

(In French, the name of the color always comes after the noun.)

c'est une pomme rouge
say-t-ëwn pohm   roož
it's a red apple

(The gender of the adjective is always the same as the noun.)

c'est une maison   blanche   (maison–feminine)
say-t-ëwn mayzohng blahngsh   (blanche–feminine)
this is a white house

voici   un papillon   blanc   (papillon–masculine)
vwahsee uhng pahpeeyohng blahng   (blanc–masculine)
here is a white butterfly

quelle jolie   couleur!
kehl   žolee kooluhr
what a pretty color!

de quelle couleur est la fleur?   (singular)
duh kehl   kooluhr ay lah fluhr
(of) what color   is the flower?

de quelles couleurs sont les fleurs?   (plural)
duh kehl   kooluhr sohng lay fluhr
(of) what colors   are the flowers?

quelle est ta   couleur   préferée?
kehl   ay tah kooluhr prayfehray
what is your favorite color?

merci,   merci   beaucoup
mehrsee, mehrsee   bokoo
thank you, thank you very much

il n'y a pas de quoi
eel nee-ah pah duh kwah
don't mention it (you're welcome)

c'est mignon
say meenohng
that's cute

c'est joli
say žolee
that's pretty

c'est beau
say bo
that's beautiful/handsome

tu es mignon   (masc.)
tëw eh meenohng
you are cute

tu es mignonne   (fem.)
tëw eh meenohn
you are cute

31

tu es joli (e)   (masc./fem. pronounced the same)
tëw eh žolee
you are pretty

tu   es beau
tëw eh bo
you are handsome

tu es belle
tëw eh behl
you are beautiful

tu as bien   fait
tëw ah byanḡ   feh
you did (well) a good job

je suis fière de toi
zuh sëwee feeyehr duh twah
I   am   proud of you

Some common forms of endearment:

mon   petit poussin
mohnḡ puhtee poosanḡ
my   little   sweetie (my little chick)

mon   petit chou
mohnḡ puhtee shoo
my   little   sweetie (cabbage)

ma chérie   (fem.)
mah shayree
my darling

mon   cheri   (masc.)
mohnḡ shayree
my   darling

mon   petit   amour   (masc. or fem.)
mohnḡ puhtee-t-ahmoor
my   little   love

mon   petit   garçon
mohnḡ puhtee gahrsohnḡ
my   little   boy

ma petite   fille
mah puhteet feë
my little   daughter (girl)

_____

vas-y
vah-z-ee
go ahead (go to it)

allons-y
ahlonḡ-z-ee
let's go

arrête
ahreht
stop

viens ici
vyanḡ-z-eesee
come here

va là-bas
vah lah bah
go   over there

assieds-toi
ahsyeh twah
sit   down

attrape
ahtrahp
catch

reste là
rehst lah
stay there

doucement
doosmahnḡ
softly/slowly/quietly

vite
veet
quickly/fast

plus vite
plëw veet
quicker/faster

dépêche toi
daypehsh twah
hurry up

ne pleure pas
nuh pluhr pah
don't cry

pourquoi tu pleures?
poorkwah tëw pluhr
why are   you crying?

tiens ma main
tyanḡ mah manḡ
hold my hand

ne touche pas
nuh toosh pah
don't touch

ne bouge pas
nuh boož pah
don't move

sois sage
swah sahž
be good

dis "au revoir"
dee o ruhvwahr
say "goodbye"

habille toi
ahbeë twah
get dressed

aide moi
ehd mwah
help me

porte ça, s'il te plaît
pohrt sah seel tuh pleh
carry this,   please

prends ça
prahn̄g sah
take this (that)

mets ça sur la table
meh sah sëwr lah tahbl
put this on the table

on joue à cache-cache?
ohn̄g žoo ah kahsh-kahsh
let's play hide and seek

cou cou
koo koo
peek a boo

va te laver les mains
vah tuh lahvay lay man̄g
go   wash your hands

tu as les mains propres
tëw ah lay man̄g prohpr
your hands are clean

tu as les mains sales
tëw ah lay man̄g sahl
your hands are dirty

je fais ma toilette
žuh feh mah twahleht
I get washed

ton petit déjeuner est prêt
tohn̄g puhtee dayžuhnay ay preh
your breakfast is ready

ton déjeuner est prêt
tohn̄g dayžuhnay ay preh
your lunch is ready

le dîner est prêt
luh deenay ay preh
dinner is ready

à table
ah tahbl
to the table

j'ai fini
žay feenee
I am finished

bien
byan̄g
good, well

très bien
treh byan̄g
very good, very well

s'il te plaît
seel tuh pleh
please

merci
mehrsee
thank you

merci beaucoup
mehrsee bokoo
thank you very much

je t'en prie
žuh t-ahn̄g pree
you are welcome

il n'y a pas de quoi
eel nee-ah pah duh kwah
think nothing of it (you're welcome)

fais dodo
feh dodo
go sleepy byes

dors bien
dohr byan̄g
sleep well

fais de beaux rêves
feh duh bo rehv
(make) sweet dreams

33

SOME USEFUL VERB CONJUGATIONS

être	**avoir**	**regarder**	**aller**
ehtr	*ahvwahr*	*ruhgahrday*	*ahlay*
to be	**to have**	**to look, to look at**	**to go**
je suis	j'ai	je regarde	je vais
žuh sëwee	*žay*	*žuh ruhgahrd*	*žuh veh*
I am	I have	I am looking	I am going
tu es	tu as	tu regardes (familiar)	tu vas (familiar)
tëw eh	*tëw ah*	*tëw ruhgahrd*	*tëw vah*
you are	you have	you look	you are going
il est	il a	il regarde	il va
eel eh	*eel ah*	*eel ruhgahrd*	*eel vah*
he is	he has	he is looking	he is going
elle est	elle a	elle regarde	elle va
ehl eh	*ehl ah*	*ehl ruhgahrd*	*ehl vah*
she is	she has	she looks	she is going
nous sommes	nous avons	nous regardons	nous allons
noo sohm	*noo-z-ahvohn̄g*	*noo ruhgahrdohn̄g*	*noo-z-ahlohn̄g*
we are	we have	we are looking	we are going
vous êtes	vous avez	vous regardez (formal or plural)	vous allez (formal or plural)
voo-z-eht	*voo-z-ahvay*	*voo ruhgahrday*	*voo-z-ahlay*
you are	you have	you look	you are going
ils sont (masc.)	ils ont (masc.)	ils regardent (masc.)	ils vont (masc.)
eel sohn̄g	*eel-z-ohn̄g*	*eel ruhgahrd*	*eel vohn̄g*
they are	they have	they look	they are going
elles sont (fem.)	elles ont (fem.)	elles regardent (fem.)	elle vont (fem.)
ehl sohn̄g	*ehl-z-ohn̄g*	*ehl ruhgahrd*	*ehl vohn̄g*
they are	they have	they look	they are going

Keep A Record Of Your Child's Progress

Child's Name_____

Age_____

Date(s)_____

Notes:

OTHER OPTIMALEARNING® PRODUCTS AVAILABLE

The OptimaLearning Classics™

This 6-tape collection consists of excerpts from magnificent classical music compositions, uniquely sequenced by Dr. Ivan Barzakov, with a variation of tempos, keys and themes to fulfill a wide variety of needs. The music has been carefully researched in Austria, Bulgaria, and North America. These singular cassettes help improve absorption, concentration and retention, foster creativity, and promote super-productivity and well being.

The OptimaLearning Classics are for everyone. You don't have to be musically inclined – just try the suggested music. Make it part of your life. You will feel the difference! These cassettes are to be used widely, at home (especially with children), school, hospitals, senior centers, medical offices, business settings.

A wonderful gift idea for family, friends, colleagues. Each cassette is 60 minutes of pure music. Easy step-by-step written instructions included. Fully guaranteed; if not completely satisfied return for exchange or refund within 30 days.

Baroque Music for Learning & Relaxation

Volume I	#301	*Composers include Handel, Locatelli, Manfredini, Pachebel, Scarlatti, Vivaldi*
Volume II	#302	*Composers include Corelli and Albinoni*

Improve memory and comprehension; facilitate test taking and problem solving; empower teaching, training and presentations of any kind; speed up convalescence; benefit pre/post natal conditions and child raising; render relaxation and therapy more effective.

Volumes III and IV available July 1994.

Music for Optimal Performance

Volume I	#401	*Special excerpts from Mozart and Vivaldi*
Volume II	#402	*Special excerpts from Bach & Rossini*

Optimize mental and physical performance; generate ideas in homework, exam preparation, organizing, writing, lab work. Energize physical exercise, routine work and daily tasks.

Music for Imagination & Creativity

Volume I	#501	*Wagner, Grieg, Ravel, Dvorák, Smetana*
Volume II	#502	*Berlioz, Debussy, Borodin, Glinka, Scriabin*

Stimulate creativity and intuition in almost any mental activity; develop visualization abilities for writing and artistic endeavors, promote effective problem solving and inventive decisions; empower contemplation, storytelling; uplift mood and help overcoming grief and loss, bring inspiration.

Adult Language Courses

Each Accelerated Learning™ course consists of twelve cassettes (one for each lesson) and a full textbook. This excellent language course will enable you to reach a good fluency quickly and easily. May also be used as a review.

Available in French, Spanish, German, Italian. ESL (Inglés)

From OptimaLearning Language Land™

Spanish For Kids™

French For Kids™

English For Kids™

"The OptimaLearning Classics cassettes have had a magical effect on the memory and creativity of not only my students, but my whole family as well."

Leo Wood, Tempe, Arizona
Chemistry teacher, father of four

For more information, write to The OptimaLearning Co., 885 Olive Avenue, Suite A, Novato, CA 94945